Law at Work

- facts no trade unionist, personnel officer, employer or employee should ignore
- concise, easy-to-read style
- assumes no previous knowledge of law
- emphasis on everyday situations in the workplace

Occupational Pensions

The creation of a company pension scheme involves a number of different interests: not least, the State in seeing its basic statutory scheme implemented; the pension fund managers who will perhaps contract out of part of the State scheme and administer a private scheme; and the employees for whose benefit it is created, together with their union representatives who will negotiate on their behalf. It is essential that all these should know the extent of the legal controls.

AUSTRALIA
The Law Book Company Ltd.
Sydney : Melbourne : Brisbane

CANADA AND U.S.A.
The Carswell Company Ltd.
Agincourt, Ontario

INDIA
N.M. Tripathi Private Ltd.
Bombay
and
Eastern Law House Private Ltd.
Calcutta
M.P.P. House
Bangalore

ISRAEL
Steimatzky's Agency Ltd.
Jerusalem : Tel Aviv : Haifa

MALAYSIA : SINGAPORE : BRUNEI
Malayan Law Journal (Pte.) Ltd.
Singapore

NEW ZEALAND
Sweet and Maxwell (N.Z.) Ltd.
Auckland

PAKISTAN
Pakistan Law House
Karachi

Abbreviations

ACAS	Advisory Conciliation and Arbitration Service
CAC	Central Arbitration Committee
CPIC	Company Pensions Information Centre
CBI	Confederation of British Industry
DHSS	Department of Health and Social Security
EAT	Employment Appeal Tribunal
EOC	Equal Opportunities Commission
EEC	European Economic Community
GAD	Government Actuary's Department
GMP	Guaranteed Minimum Pension
HMSO	Her Majesty's Stationery Office
NAPF	National Association of Pension Funds
OPB	Occupational Pensions Board
RPI	Retail Price Index
SFO	Superannuation Fund Office
TUC	Trades Union Congress

General Editor of the Series: Paul O'Higgins, M.A., Ph.D.
Advisory Editor: John Broadbent, M.A.

Other Titles in the Series

Discipline
Dismissal
Employment Contracts
Going to Law
Health and Safety
Job Security
Safety Representatives
Sex Discrimination
Social Security
Trade Disputes
Trade Unions
Union Members
Wages and Salaries

1 Introduction

Why should a series entitled "Law at Work" include a book on occupational pension schemes? The simple answer is that company pensions are becoming increasingly important to a growing number of working people since they represent a significant, though often hidden, element of an employee's remuneration. Trade unions therefore take a much greater interest in such private schemes than before, and the subject is becoming an accepted area for collective bargaining within our industrial relations framework. Member participation in the running of pension schemes is probably more favourably viewed nowadays; and, with the recently improved State scheme and emphasis on contracting-out, more questions are being asked generally about the control, management, and public accountability of private schemes.

On the other hand, it has to be accepted immediately that the setting up and running of a scheme is an extremely complicated matter, heavily dependent upon expert advice, particularly from actuaries and investment advisers. This complexity is reflected in the law which governs them. So to be understandable to the non-specialist the legal and financial aspects have to be considerably simplified; but it must be remembered that a simplified account such as this is only a guide, and if any particular problem arises with a scheme or a member's entitlement under it, the actual detailed laws or rules should be consulted, and expert advice sought.

As we shall see, pension funds have become one of the major institutions in the modern financial world, and certainly one of the most important forms of institutional savings. Very large amounts of money are involved. In 1975 it was estimated that pension funds had 11.5 million members, an annual income of £6,200 million, and annual expenditure of £2,700 million. As well as being a fertile source of investment money, they may also have a definite levelling effect on the distribution of income in our society. The Diamond Commission on the Distribution of Income and Wealth (which was dissolved in 1979) produced the following figures for 1976, showing the effect of including pension entitlements in assessing personal wealth:

Population	*Share of marketable wealth (£274 bn.)*	*Share with occupational rights added (£324 bn.)*	*Share with occupational and State pension rights added (£505 bn.)*
Richest 1%	25 %	21 %	14 %
2—5%	21 %	20 %	15 %
6—10%	14 %	14 %	11 %
11—20%	17 %	17 %	15 %
Bottom 80%	23 %	28 %	45 %

As well as a discussion of the different aspects of the law covering pension schemes, this book includes a certain amount of basic statistical material, mainly in order to illustrate the size and realities of the subject. There are two major sources of such material. One is the Government Actuary's 1975 Survey of Pension Funds. The other is the National Association of Pension Funds' 1979 Survey of Occupational Pension Schemes; this survey is produced annually and contains much recent information. The 1979 survey does not cover all schemes. It is estimated that there are about 65,000 schemes in the United Kingdom, with 11.5 million members. The 1979 NAPF Survey only covered 1,190 schemes but, as these included most of the biggest ones, they accounted for 6 million fund members (*i.e.* over one-half of the total), and had assets totalling £33,710 million. The results of the survey therefore give a good indication of modern patterns and trends in pension schemes generally.

The arrangement of the book is to start with the State

pension scheme, and then look at the legal and financial characteristics of a private scheme. The all-important tax aspects then have to be considered since, as we shall see, it is the detailed rules insisted upon by the Inland Revenue that *shape* the characteristic scheme. We shall then look at the process of "contracting out," and at the body with overall control, the Occupational Pensions Board. Some emphasis will then be placed, in Chapter 7, on the sometimes controversial topic of member participation and the involvement of trade unions in the running of schemes. Finally, three specific legal topics will be considered: the preservation of pension rights for people who move jobs, the question of equal pension treatment for women, and the overlap between pension law and unfair dismissal (where loss of pension rights may be an important item for which compensation can be claimed). The book finishes with Appendices covering further reading and an introduction to the various organisations active in the field and their publications. Not surprisingly, this highly complicated area has produced a lot of highly specialised material. This book by contrast is written as a relatively gentle introduction.

2 The Improved State Pension Scheme

It has been commonly accepted since the beginning of this century that the State should provide at least a basic retirement pension, and this has gradually become part of the overall social security system, particularly since the post-war reforms which followed the Beveridge Report. From that time on, the system provided basic flat-rate pensions financed through national insurance contributions. Private schemes operated in addition for some people, but were not integrated into the State system.

In the late sixties and early seventies, interest grew in the possibility of improved State pensions (given that not everyone belonged to private schemes) but there was considerable disagreement as to how this should be done, leading to pensions being treated for a period as the proverbial political football. The Conservative Government introduced a plan in 1973, but this was abandoned by the Labour Government which succeeded it. Instead, that Government introduced what has become known as the "Castle Plan." This was embodied in the Social Security Pensions Act 1975, and came fully into effect in April 1978. Fortunately, it has secured a high degree of agreement among the political parties and hopefully should be allowed to settle into the long period of stability that is essential for any pensions plan.

The new scheme is to split the State pension into two parts:

(a) The basic pension. This is the basic, flat-rate pension which all earners are to get; and

(b) The "additional component." This is an additional, earnings-related amount on top of the basic pension. It reaches its maximum after 20 years in the scheme, and is calculated as a percentage of the employee's earnings in his best-paid 20 years (with past years brought up to present-day values), subject to upper limits on the amount of income that can count.

It is this additional component which is the major improvement in the State scheme. On the other hand, many employees are already in private schemes that provide additional benefits. The answer here has been to integrate the State and the private schemes by allowing private schemes to "contract out" of the additional component. This means that, in return for a decrease in national insurance contributions, the individuals under such a scheme pay into that scheme instead of the State additional component.

Contracting out is a complicated procedure with several detailed requirements and is supervised by the Occupational Pensions Board; these matters are considered in Chapter 6. One of the basic qualifications for contracting out is that the private scheme must provide a Guaranteed Minimum Pension (GMP). This is calculated by a complicated formula, but in effect it means the amount of the State additional component that the employee would have got if he had not been in contracted out employment. This notional figure of the GMP (which includes the GMP for a widow too) is found often in the many detailed and extremely complex laws and rules which surround occupational pension schemes. In practice, however, it is less important, since the aim of most contracted out private schemes is not just to be in substitution for the State scheme, but to be significantly *better.*

3 The Idea of Private Occupational Pension Schemes

The main aim of the present law on occupational pensions is to encourage employers and employees to make provision on a voluntary basis for pension benefits better than those provided under the State pension scheme. This was clearly important when the State only provided the flat-rate old age pension. With the coming of the new State pension scheme the matter becomes more complicated, but that does not make private schemes less important. What it does do is to make the *relationship* between State and private pensions more important. Basically, a private scheme may either participate in the State scheme by providing certain benefits *in addition* to those provided by the new State pension laws, *or* it may "contract out" on the State scheme altogether, so that it *replaces* the additional pension element, usually on a more generous basis. Most schemes choose to contract out, which means that the employer and employee pay less into the State scheme, and the employee receives only the basic pension from the State, not the additional element.

The procedure for contracting out is considered in Chapter 6. It gives independent trade unions certain rights to be consulted over the decision whether to contract out. In practice, however, the widespread existence of private pension schemes has led to much greater union involvement, not confined to the contracting-out decision. Unions are active, for instance, in negotiating over the setting up of pension funds, and on the improvement of benefits from existing funds. Moreover, the modern tendency is towards having member representatives on the governing bodies of pension funds, as member trustees, though here it is easy to stray into highly contentious areas, as we shall see in Chapter 7.

Private schemes have become a major financial institution in this country, being found commonly in both the private and the public sectors of British industry and employment. It has been estimated that there are about 65,000 occupational pension schemes in the United Kingdom with about 11.5 million members (i.e. half of the total working population of 23 million). This membership figure shows an imbalance of the sexes—8.7 million men and 2.8 million women—and we shall look at the law on sex discrimination, as it applies to pension schemes, in Chapter 9. In the meantime, we shall look in this chapter at the characteristics of a modern occupational pension scheme and at the problem of inflation.

Characteristics of a scheme

We shall see in Chapter 5 that modern pension schemes must be made to fit into a whole series of complicated tax laws. This is because such schemes can only be financially worth while if they claim the wide exemption from various taxes (income tax, capital gains tax, capital transfer tax) that are available under those laws *if* a scheme complies with certain very definite requirements insisted upon by the Inland Revenue. It is therefore the tax rules more than anything else that mould the present day pension scheme into its characteristic form.

What does such a scheme look like? First of all, schemes may cater for different types of employees. Essentially, a scheme may be a staff scheme, a works scheme or a combined scheme. In addition, it is increasingly common to have either a separate scheme or a "topping-up" scheme for directors and senior management. Thus a large firm may have different schemes in operation at the same time.

The large majority of funds are "contributory," *i.e.* the employee must contribute towards them out of his earnings. The National Association of Pension Funds' 1979 survey found that the average contribution rate for employees was 4¾ per cent. of earnings for staff schemes and 3¾ per cent. of earnings for works schemes. The larger share of the contribution to the fund, however, comes from the employer, and here the 1979 survey found that the average contribution rate from the employer was 13 per cent. of earnings for staff schemes and 7¾ per cent. of earnings for works schemes. This is an important hidden cost of employment for an employer who maintains a private pension scheme, and it is an area open to union involvement and negotiation.

The retirement age for the majority of schemes remains at the normal retirement age of 65 for a man and 60 for a woman, though this might well prove to be an area for change in the future. In Chapter 9 we shall look at the effect (or rather, lack of effect) of the sex discrimination laws on this age difference.

The usual way to calculate the retirement pension payable is by reference to the pensioner's length of service with the employer. This is normally done by allowing a fraction of salary for each year of continuous employment. The two most usual fractions are one-eightieth or, in more generous schemes, one-sixtieth. In the case of the latter, there will normally be a rule that a maximum of 40 years can be counted, so that the maximum pension is forty-sixtieths, *i.e.* two-thirds of salary (the maximum allowed by the Inland Revenue for an "approved scheme"—see Chapter 5).

The generosity or otherwise of a pension entitlement may depend not just on the fraction per year of service, but also on the "salary" figure which is used for calculation purposes. Naturally, in nominal value, the salary of a person about to retire will have risen dramatically over the years he has been employed. On the other hand, it may be that in *real* terms his salary has fluctuated considerably over the years (for example, where he has been paid by results). Which figure should be used as the "base" figure by which to calculate the pension entitlement? It is possible to work out a "career average" (*i.e.* an employee's average salary throughout his career), but that method is not used extensively. The practical answer in most modern schemes is to use the retiring employee's "final salary" or "final average salary." The latter can be worked out in many different ways, all depending on which particular formula the scheme in question has chosen. It could be, for example, the average salary over the final year, or final three or five years, or the average salary over the best three-year period in the final 10 years. The NAPF 1979 survey found that, in the schemes surveyed, this last formula of the best three years out of the last 10 was the most common (36 per cent. of schemes surveyed); 38 per cent. of schemes took a straight average over a final period covering from one to five years, and only 7 per cent. took the actual salary on retirement. The final salary formula is clearly in the interests of someone whose salary continues to rise in real terms up to the moment of retirement, though someone whose real income fluctuates may be better off under a scheme which takes a longer-term average. Either way, it will be an important factor for an employee planning his retirement; for example, someone with an option to retire early may have to weigh the disadvantage in leisure terms of working for a couple of years longer against the advantage in pension terms that may come through working for those extra years to reach a higher final salary.

In addition to providing a regular pension during retirement, a scheme may also allow a retiring employee to take part of his pension entitlement as a lump sum. Provided that this stays within the Inland Revenue's requirements (which principally means a maximum lump sum of one-and-a-half times final remuneration), this amount will be tax free. Ninety per cent. of schemes covered by the NAPF 1979 survey offered members such lump sum "commutations"; and there was no significant difference here between staff and works schemes.

Benefits will normally also be provided where the member dies in service or after retirement. Where death occurs in service, most schemes give a lump sum (often of two to two-and-a-half times salary) *and* a widow's pension, most commonly of half the member's pension (the maximum allowable by the Inland Revenue being two-thirds). Death in retirement normally entitles the widow to a pension; the 1979 survey found that in 88 per cent. of schemes surveyed this was half of the member's pension.

The problem of inflation

It is quite obvious that one of the major effects of a continued period of high inflation is to decrease the real value of savings funds, and thereby to make advanced planning of such funds very difficult. Two particular problems arise with pension schemes—how to maintain the pension entitlement at a realistic level throughout the member's period of employment, and how to ensure that pensions being paid to pensioners are increased to keep their real value in times of inflation.

The first problem—maintenance of the entitlement—arises because the employee's wages keep going up, but of course his "entitlement" is built up over the years, stretching back to a time when, in money terms, he was earning much less. This does not pose problems if his pension is eventually calculated on his final salary, since this will probably reflect the effects of inflation. However, where the pension is calculated on any sort of *average* salary over a period of years (for example, by taking the best three years in the last 10, which we saw above is quite a common formula), then the employee could lose out if inflation were not taken into account, since in those past years he will have earned *less* in money terms, even if he was just as well off in real terms. The answer will be for a scheme which uses an average salary formula to take inflation into account (at least to a certain extent) by notionally increasing back years' pay by a set amount, to reach the modern-day equivalent of the real value of that pay. This can be done by the scheme's actuaries, and the Inland Revenue will accept this form of "enhancement" (sometimes called a "dynamised" final average salary) provided the increase is, at most, in line with increases in the Retail Price Index (which measures rises in the cost of living). It must be remembered, however, that these increases in entitlements have to be paid for, since contributions in the past will have been based on the *actual* pay rates at that time, not on the artificially enhanced pay rates; in other words, the fund will have to find the money from somewhere, either from its income or from additional payments in. As we shall see in Chapter 8, this sort of operation also has to be carried out in the case of people who leave employment and are entitled to a deferred (or "frozen") pension, in order to keep up their entitlements.

The second problem concerns increasing the amount of pensions once they have started to be paid. If an employee retired 10 years ago on £x per week, he will now need considerably more than that simply to keep the same standard of living—the exercise in running hard to stay in the same place that is so common in inflationary times. The ideal answer is index-linking, *i.e.* fixing the pension so that it increases automatically in line with a particular standard, such as the Retail Prices Index; this should ensure that the real value of the pension remains stable in spite of inflation. It is however expensive to do, and it is not surprising that only a tiny proportion of schemes in the private sector are index-linked. It is different in the public sector where many pensions for ex-public employees, such as civil servants, are index-linked. This can cause some controversy in inflationary times. The present Government appear to be hostile to continuing this particular benefit, and while (at the time of writing) there are no immediate plans for legislation to end it, such a development is possible. It certainly seems that, if civil servants are to retain this benefit, they are likely to have to pay more for it, by means of an increased employee contribution.

In the private sector, the picture is very different. Of the private sector schemes covered by the NAPF 1979 survey, 64 per cent. did not have any provision for automatic increases in pensions; of the 36 per cent. which did, only 1 per cent. increased them in line with the R.P.I., and the majority of them gave increases of between 3-4 per cent. per annum only. Ironically, it may therefore be better to belong to a scheme which does *not* automatically increase pensions by a set figure, for in such a scheme there is a chance of the trustees deciding that they can in fact pay more in any given year than they would have been prepared to commit themselves to in advance. This is certainly the case with the larger pension schemes, some of which have managed successfully to keep up with inflation, even though not index-linked and not tied to automatic increases (the ICI pension fund, for example). This may be partly due to the fact that larger funds tend to be privately invested rather than run through insurance companies, and certain forms of investment are more able than others to keep up with inflation. However, this sort of practical inflation proofing is by no means certain in smaller funds and this factor (when taken along with the large number of schemes making automatic increases of well below the annual increase in the RPI) must be a cause for concern. Inflation is therefore a major worry for pensioner and pension fund manager alike. The worst prospect is of sustained high inflation eventually meaning that pension funds could in theory become insupportable by the amount of contributions being paid in. Likewise, high inflation, rapidly eroding the real value of private pensions, could eventually mean that such schemes were no longer better than the ordinary State scheme (which operates on a "pay-as-you-go" basis), and so the whole purpose of the occupational pension system would have been defeated. However, this has not happened yet, and fears that it may should not detract from the otherwise great advantages of having fully funded private schemes, although the costs and difficulties of maintaining such funds in inflationary times should not be underestimated. If the time ever did come when hyper-inflation totally destroyed the viability of pension funds, we should all be too busy withdrawing our bank balances in wheelbarrows and growing our own cabbages to notice.

4 The Legal Basis and Financing of a Private Scheme

Legal basis

We have said that a fund must obtain certain tax concessions if it is to operate properly, and to obtain them it must satisfy certain very definite requirements laid down by the Inland Revenue. It is this factor that gives schemes many of the characteristics which they have in common, as we saw in the last chapter. This in turn means that the drafting of a scheme is very important, and it is here that legal advice and expertise may be needed.

In order to satisfy the Inland Revenue, one of the requirements is that the scheme must be permanent. This is done by establishing it as a trust, under a trust deed with a set of rules which govern its administration. The pension scheme is therefore in law something entirely separate from the employer (whether that employer is a person, firm or company), administered separately from the employer's business and not under the control of the employer.

As a trust, the pension fund will be controlled by trustees who will usually be given a large measure of discretion as to how to run the scheme. In one area, this discretion is particularly important. In order to make sure that any payments made by the fund on the occasion of a pensioner's death are not caught by capital transfer tax, those payments (for example to the widow or other dependants) must be made at the trustees' *discretion,* not as a *right*. The common form of providing for this in the trust deed is for the trustees to be given this discretion; but for them unofficially to ask each member of the scheme to fill out a

"Declaration of Wish," stating whom he would *like* to receive the money. In practice, the trustees will put this wish into effect when he dies, so it is important for the member to make sure that the form in question accurately represents his real intentions. The importance of this aspect of a pension scheme needs no overemphasis nowadays when in practice the two most valuable assets left by many people on their death will be their house and any rights they have under a pension scheme.

Another important area for the trustees' discretion will concern the way the fund is to be invested and managed. It is obvious that a scheme can only exist by making gains from its investments, so this will be one of the trustees' most important functions, though, naturally, they will rely heavily on expert advice in making investment decisions. To assist them in this duty, it is common for the trust deed to give them very wide powers of investment. If this is not done, their investment powers will be governed by a statute (the Trustee Investments Act 1961) which places rather stricter limits on what they can and cannot put fund money into.

The office of trustee is well known to the law in all sorts of contexts, and many legal rules have grown up which strictly apply to it. Thus, a trustee must comply exactly with the terms of the trust, invest wisely and lawfully, keep proper records and be prepared to produce information. Moreover, a trustee must act fairly and honestly; in particular, he must not make personal profits out of the trust, and must not discriminate improperly between the people who are entitled to benefit under the trust ("beneficiaries"). The trustee is accountable to a high degree for his actions, or lack of them.

The reason for stating these principles here is that there can sometimes be misunderstandings about what the position of pension fund trustee means, particularly in a scheme which has provisions allowing for member representation, *i.e.* a certain number of trustees to be appointed from, or elected by, the employees actually paying into the fund. We shall see in Chapter 7 that pension rights are now accepted as an area for union negotiation, which may mean, among other things, union pressure for representation of member employees on the board of trustees of the scheme. However, that does not alter a trustee's duties and obligations once put on to the board. He must still act fairly, responsibly and impartially, within the confines of the realistic financial position of the scheme. In law, it is quite wrong for a person to be appointed or elected as a trustee on the basis that he is going to raise benefits as a matter of principle, or benefit one class of members at the expense of another, or seek radical changes in investment policy. Trusteeship is above all a legal office, not a political one. Perhaps a parallel can be drawn here with the laymen on an industrial tribunal—they are selected from panels drawn up by employers and unions, but once selected they are supposed to act as impartial judges in any particular case, not as partisan representatives of their "side."

The legal aspects of a pension fund are therefore important, at least when setting it up. However, the day-to-day running of a scheme is basically a financial matter, heavily dependent on expert advice from pensions experts such as actuaries, accountants and insurance company representatives, rather than lawyers. It is to that financial side that we must now turn.

Financing

There are in theory two ways of financing a scheme. One is by *funding,* that is to say by accumulating funds throughout the life of the scheme (by employer and employee contributions), and investing or insuring those funds so that there are ample resources from which to pay out the pensions as they become due. The other way is "pay-as-you-go," which is where there are no accumulated funds, but pensions due to be paid in any given year are paid out of the contributions paid into the scheme in that year by those members who are still working. The State pension scheme works on the latter ("cash flow") basis; but in this country, almost all private occupational pensions schemes are funded.

Given that pension schemes, by their very nature, operate in the long term, it does not need any stretching of the imagination to realise the huge amounts of money that are involved (see Chap. 1). Pension funds are now a major source of investment finance. This raises three main points: the solvency of a pension scheme, its form of administration, and the way it invests its funds.

(a) *Solvency*

As with any major financial institution, the financial reliability (or "solvency") of a pension fund is of crucial importance, particularly to the employees who are paying into it. The prospect of a pension fund folding up or going bankrupt is one that would rightly horrify its members. In its 1975 report *Solvency, disclosure of information and member participation in occupational pension schemes,* the Occupational Pensions Board (OPB) found that, of late, there has been great stability and reliability in the running of pension schemes. However, that certainly does not mean that further checks are unnecessary. In fact, the OPB is given, by law, far-reaching powers to scrutinise pension schemes to ensure that they are fully solvent, and being run in a way which will ensure that they have sufficient funds to be able to meet their obligations in full. To this end, funds have to provide detailed financial information to the OPB, to be checked on a regular basis. If the OPB finds that a scheme is under-funded, it has power to order the employer to inject more funds into the scheme to make good the shortfall. If the employer fails to do so, the OPB can recover the money in question directly from the employer under special legal powers, and can also threaten to withdraw the contracted-out certificate.

In addition, the OPB has powers to monitor the investment policy of the fund. It can ensure that too much money is not placed into any one investment, since the crash of that investment could seriously endanger the fund's solvency; and it can keep an eye on what is called "self-investment," *i.e.* investment by the fund back into the employer's business which, again, might be financially unstable. Up to a point, this kind of investment might be mutually beneficial to employer and fund, but limits are placed on it by the OPB, in the longer-term interests of the fund.

The OPB is also undertaking further study of the whole question of solvency, and whether further safeguards are necessary.

(b) *Administration.*

Apart from pension schemes specially set up by statute for certain public employees, the majority of schemes are in the private sector, and here the OPB uses a twofold classification: *insured* schemes and *self-administered* schemes.

Insured schemes are those where the trustees in effect delegate the responsibility for meeting the scheme's liabilities by buying insurance cover from an insurance company which agrees to pay the pensions as they become due in return for premiums from the scheme. It is then up to the insurance company to make enough money from those premiums to pay out the pensions. *Self-administered schemes* are those where the trustees themselves administer the fund and its assets, remaining responsible for the investment policy and the eventual payment of the pensions; however it must be noted that in practice the majority of these schemes (sometimes called "managed funds") will rely for detailed advice on an external fund manager, which may well be an insurance company. The trend is clearly towards more schemes being self-administered and certainly the larger a scheme is, the more likely it is to be self-administered.
The overall position can be seen from the table below, which is taken from the 1979 survey by the National Association of Pension Funds, to whom the author is indebted for their kind permission to reproduce it.

Table—Investment Medium

	Staff Schemes	Works Schemes	Combined Schemes	All Schemes
	%	%	%	%
Insured	27	23	18	23
Privately Invested	57	59	70	63
Mixed—Insured/Invested	3	2	2	3
Insurance Managed Fund Units	12	15	10	12
Unfunded	—	1	—	—
TOTAL	99	100	100	101

(c) *Investments*

The importance of pension funds in the modern financial world is clear. However, the actual range of investment of a fund could be a matter for some controversy, and this is likely to be increasingly so. Any investment scheme has to have a certain amount of diversification to be secure (in case one particular investment fails), and part of its pattern of investments has to be "safe," probably in fixed-interest securities which yield a stable, if modest, return. To keep pace in times of inflation, however, there may be pressure on a fund to go in for investments with a higher return although in the nature of things these may tend to be more risky. Moreover, there may be certain kinds of investment which do not produce income at all, but even so are in themselves a good hedge against inflation, since their *value* goes up. We have therefore seen some pension funds becoming important customers in the market for land, buildings, art works and antiques. The British Rail pension fund in particular has figured in the news because of its art purchases.

It is certainly true that the larger the scheme, the more likely it is to invest in property (such as land and buildings) as well as stocks and shares. However, questions of the best overall balance of investments for any particular fund, and of how adventurous or otherwise an investment policy should be, may be difficult ones for the trustees or managers, particularly in times of inflationary pressure not just to keep up the level of funding in the scheme, but to increase the levels of pensions already being paid in order to give some protection to the pensioners.

5 Taxation Aspects

It is certainly true that the present tax laws relating to occupational pension schemes are very complicated (even after the "simplification" in 1970), so that anyone involved in the practical management of a pension fund must always keep an eye open for the taxation aspects to anything he may be thinking of doing, and must be prepared to seek good professional advice. One additional complexity in this specialised area is that, as we shall see, a great deal of *discretion* is left to the Inland Revenue by the legislation, and that means that often it is necessary to know not only what the law says, but also what practices the Inland Revenue have adopted.

Ever since 1921, tax law has made various allowances and exceptions in favour of occupational pension schemes, provided such schemes had the approval of the Inland Revenue. At first, their approval was necessary mainly to make sure that pension schemes were not being used as means of tax avoidance (by allowing employers to store up large amounts of money in tax-free funds, or by allowing employees to get additional tax-free "wages" which they could later withdraw from the scheme). It is certainly arguable that today the purpose of granting Inland Revenue approval is different—today, it is at least partly as a way of controlling the *operation* of pension funds in the interests of members and of society generally. This view certainly gains strength when the powers of the Occupational Pensions Board (see the next chapter) are considered alongside the more purely financial powers of the Inland Revenue.

Not surprisingly, the laws relating to pension schemes

have become ever more complicated, as indeed has the whole of tax law. The Finance Act 1970 (ss. 19 to 26) attempted to simplify the position by introducing the "New Code" (which, amongst other things, removed certain detailed restrictions, for example restrictions on directors belonging to schemes); this code finally came into full effect in April 1980 by which time all schemes had to comply with it. The tax laws relating to pension funds are administered separately by the Inland Revenue's Superannuation Fund Office (SFO) which shares premises at New Malden with the Occupational Pensions Board (see Appendix 1). The functions of these two bodies are, as we shall see, different, but obviously there is a considerable overlap between them.

Although the actual tax laws in question are complicated, the simple point is that a pension scheme needs the special tax treatment if it is to operate economically, and to get that special treatment it must be accepted by the SFO as what is called an "exempt approved" scheme. We must therefore look first at what tax reliefs are available, and secondly at how a scheme qualifies as "exempt approved."

The special tax treatment

Under modern tax law, liability to pay various taxes can arise in various ways, but usually they have in common that either some property or money is passed from one person to another, or there is some definable gain made somewhere along the line. Pension schemes mean, by their very nature, that money (or rights to it) is constantly being made over from one person to another, and of course the scheme can only exist by making gains from wise investments. Thus, potentially there are many ways in which the scheme, or the employer, or the employee (or, knowing the way tax law operates, all three!) could become liable to one tax or another. This is why the tax reliefs which are allowed to exempt approved schemes are so vital.

To give a couple of examples, if there were no exemptions it is likely that the contributions paid into a scheme by an employer would be treated by the Revenue as part of the employee's *wages* (albeit a hidden part), and so the employee would have to pay income tax on them, even though they at no point passed through his hands. Likewise, he would have to pay full income tax on the contributions which he himself paid into the scheme. Moreover, when the scheme itself made investment gains it would probably have to pay over a significant proportion to the Revenue as capital gains tax. As a final example, benefits paid over to a widow on the pensioner's death would be at risk of being liable to capital transfer tax. The aim of the legislation is therefore to put exempt approved pension schemes into a protected position in all of these ways.

The main tax advantages of such a scheme are as follows:

(i) Employer contributions to the scheme are not treated as part of the employee's income for income tax purposes.
(ii) The employer can deduct his contributions to the scheme from his taxable income, as a business expense.
(iii) The employee gets tax relief on his deductions to the scheme (this being done automatically through the PAYE system).
(iv) The pension scheme itself is free from tax on income from investments and from capital gains tax. (Note, however, that it is not free from tax on any income from commercial trading).
(v) Payments made by the trustees to a pensioner's dependants on his death (*e.g.* to his widow) are not subject to capital transfer tax, provided the payments are made at the trustees' *discretion*, and not by the direction of the late pensioner (hence the importance of the "declaration of wish" form which gives the trustees guidance on how to exercise their discretion, but does not force them to pay the money involved to a particular person).

What is an "exempt approved" scheme?

In theory, this entails two elements: being "exempt" and

being "approved". To be exempt, the scheme must already be approved; but in addition the Revenue must be satisfied that is is also established under what are called "irrevocable trusts." This is a way of saying that the arrangement must be of a permanent nature. This is why the scheme will normally be set up formally with a trust deed and a set of rules.

Much more important is the requirement that the scheme must be approved. The legal set-up here seems at first sight rather strange, but certainly succeeds in what is presumably its aim, *i.e.* to give the Revenue an extremely wide discretionary power of approval. Under the Finance Act 1970, s. 19, a scheme can *demand* to be approved if it meets certain criteria. However, these criteria are drafted so restrictively that most schemes will not want to abide by them. Instead, they will proceed under section 20, which gives the Revenue *discretionary* power to approve schemes even if they do not qualify under section 19. This is a very wide power, the exercise of which would be very difficult to challenge in a court of law. However, the SFO does give definite guidance on the way in which it will normally exercise its discretion, *i.e.* on what sort of schemes it is likely in practice to approve. It must be stressed, however, that ultimately the Revenue is not bound by this guidance, and it is always open to them to take a different approach if they think the circumstances demand it.

The guidance in question is contained in the Inland Revenue publication IR 12 "Occupational Pension Schemes," usually known as the Practice Notes. This is published by the SFO, and was last revised in 1979. It runs to 94 pages, mostly of detailed requirements for approval. For the details in any particular case, IR 12 must be consulted, but in general the main requirements for discretionary approval are as follows:

(i) The employer must contribute to the scheme.

(ii) The maximum amount which the employee may contribute is 15 per cent. of his salary (though in practice the average employee contribution is much less than that, as we saw in Chap. 3).

(iii) The pension must provide at least the guaranteed minimum pension, and must be based on the employee's final salary, or final average salary. Other forms of calculation may be allowable (e.g. career average schemes), but may be subject to more scrutiny by the Revenue to make sure that they do not produce excessive benefits. Where the calculation depends on averaging certain back-years or looking back at salary over a period of years, the actual figures of salary earned must be increased in line with cost of living increases to bring them up to present-day equivalents. This produces what is called "dynamised final remuneration."

(iv) The maximum pension is two-thirds of final remuneration after 40 or more years of service. There is no actual maximum figure, provided the pension in question stays within this formula. Any lump sum must be included in the calculation.

(v) Any (tax free) lump sum given out of the pension entitlement on retirement must be no greater than one-and-a-half times final remuneration.

(vi) Death benefits are subject to maximum amounts; in particular the widow's benefit can only be two-thirds of the pension.

(vii) Early retirement before 50 is not allowed, except in the case of ill health.

There are of course other detailed requirements for approval. However, it can be seen from those listed here that it is the need for Revenue approval, and the discretionary rules relating to that approval, that give pension schemes most of their essential characteristics, which we saw briefly in Chapter 3. If a scheme does not comply with the Revenue's requirements, approval may be withheld, with dire consequences. Likewise, if a scheme which is approved alters later so that it no longer meets the above requirements in some way, approval may be withdrawn. Finally, it should be noted that although the Occupational Pensions Board does not have direct powers to withdraw the privileged tax status, it is unlikely that any scheme which did not meet OPB requirements (for example, on preservation rights or equal access) would be approved by the SFO under their discretionary powers.

6 Contracting Out and the Powers of the Occupational Pensions Board

The meaning of "contracting out"

We saw in Chapter 2 that, as from 1978, the State pension scheme has been much improved, so that it is no longer limited to the flat-rate basic pension, but now also includes the earnings-related "additional component." However, it is still not as generous as many potential pensioners might wish, and so the emphasis is still clearly upon private schemes run by employers to improve upon the State benefits. It is possible for employers and employees to arrange to do this by paying fully into the State scheme, but at the same time establishing a small private scheme to "top up" the eventual pensions. However, it is much more common for a private scheme to go the whole way and "contract out" of the new additional component of the State scheme altogether. This means that the employee will only receive the basic pension from the State, but will have the benefit of the occupational pension on top of that. Employers and employees in a contracted-out scheme of course pay lower national insurance contributions in respect of pensions. The aim, it must be remembered, is to provide in practice a pension which is not just in substitution for the State's additional component, but rather is substantially *better* (how much better being a matter for negotiation when setting up the scheme).

The decision whether or not to contract out is therefore a very basic one in the running of a pension scheme. When making it, the employer may not discriminate between employees except on the basis of different types of employment (*e.g.* staff schemes or works schemes).

The procedure for contracting out

The legislation governing contracting out (to be found mainly in the Social Security Pensions Act 1975, and various sets of regulations) sets up a procedure which tries to ensure that the people involved in the pension scheme are given full details of what is happening, and that the decision is not taken without consultation with recognised trade unions.

First of all, notices must be given to the employees concerned three months before the decision is to be made. These notices must give full details of the proposed extent of the contracting out, the benefits to be provided, the effect on State pensions, and the ways in which the employees can make representations to the employer or directly to the Occupational Pensions Board (OPB).

In addition to this notification, the employer must also give similar written particulars to all "independent trade unions recognised to any extent for the purpose of collective bargaining in relation to the earners concerned." This position is in line with much of modern labour relations law in giving legal rights to trade unions. Moreover, the employer is under a further obligation to *consult* with the unions involved over the proposed contracting out. An "independent" trade union is one which has been certified as independent of management influences (see Richard Kidner, *Trade Unions*, in this series). "Recognised" is not defined in the legislation; it has been interpreted by the courts as meaning that, in practice, there is a considerable degree of acceptance on *both* sides that the union in question is the proper negotiating body in relation to the employees in question (see *NUGSAT* v. *Allbury Bros*, 1978, a case arising in a different area of law, but the question being the same—whether a union was "recognised"—and the Court of Appeal's views on the matter applying equally to the area of pensions consultation).

If a union thinks that the employer is not abiding by these rules by failing to make bona fide attempts at consultation, or if any question arises whether a particular union is one which ought to be consulted, the union can apply to an industrial tribunal to have the matter settled. One point to notice here is that these statutory union rights only apply to the decision to contract out. They do not give rights to continued involvement in the running of the scheme once it is established. The question of member and/or union involvement is a highly contentious one, and is treated separately in the next chapter.

A further point to notice is that problems could arise over consultation where "the employer" is in fact just one subsidiary of a large group or holding company, which has one overall pension scheme for all the relevant class of employees in all of the subsidiaries. If it is this overall scheme which is to be contracted out, that can be done by one application to the OPB (rather than by separate applications by each subsidiary), and, if all of the unions agree in writing, by consultation with the holding company itself. Providing that this is done properly (and with a large group of companies there may be many unions involved) the OPB will accept this as sufficient compliance with the law.

Once all of this has been done, the employer has three months from the expiry of the original notices in which to apply to the OPB for a contracted-out certificate.

The Occupational Pensions Board and contracting out

The OPB is the body set up by statute to supervise pension schemes. Its members are appointed; and while the whole Board meets several times a year, much of its detailed work is done by committees. It has joint offices with the Inland Revenue's Superannuation Fund Office (see Chap. 5 above), and at the end of 1978 employed 127 staff. It must make an annual report on its workings; these reports, usually published in about May of the following year, are very valuable sources of information on the operation of the OPB and the whole contracting-out procedure.

Perhaps its primary function is to scrutinise applications for contracted-out status, and, if satisfied, to issue the necessary certificate to a scheme. The employer must apply to the OPB, supplying it with copies of the notices given to employees and unions, copies of the trust deeds and rules, and evidence of solvency (either from an actuary in the case of a self-administered scheme, or from an insurance company in the case of an insured scheme). The OPB must then examine the scheme to see if it passes the legal tests for contracting out. These are quite complex, but essentially mean that the scheme must:

(a) provide at least the Guaranteed Minimum Pension (GMP) for the pensioner and for his widow (on the GMP, see Chap. 2 above);
(b) satisfy certain requirements as to the calculation of benefits, in particular that the pension entitlement is based on the pensioner's final salary or a final average salary, with a minimum accrual rate of 1/80th of salary per year of contracted-out employment;
(c) be solvent, and comply with the legal rules on preservation of pension rights for early leavers (Chap. 8) and equal access for women (Chap. 9).

When the new pension laws came into effect in 1978, the OPB had to deal with a deluge of applications from existing pension funds, seeking the new legal status. The OPB's 1978 Annual Report shows that in that year it issued 21,645 contracted-out certificates.

Any later alterations to a contracted-out scheme which affect any of the above matters must be approved by the OPB, which has the power at any time to cancel an existing certificate.

Other powers of the OPB

In addition to its contracting-out duties, the OPB has a

whole range of other powers and duties to help it in its overall supervisory role. The most important are as follows:

First, the OPB has powers to order the modification or, in an extreme case, the winding up of a pension scheme. These are very wide powers, but it is likely that they will not often be used. If the OPB finds that a scheme does not comply with the legal requirements in some way, it is more likely to offer its help and advice as to how to cure the defects, and in most cases, this will produce the desired result without the OPB resorting to its powers to compel changes.

Second, the OPB may make formal "determinations" on certain questions (for example, whether a scheme complies with the equal access requirements). Once again, these will help schemes to make necessary re-arrangements. If someone still disagrees with the determination, he may ask the OPB to review it (*i.e.* to think again); but if that fails, his rights are very limited, since he can only appeal to the ordinary courts against a determination on what is called a "point of law." In essence, this means that the OPB's view can only be appealed against if the board has made some error of law or has exceeded its jurisdiction; if the complaint is about something less major than that, the OPB's decision is, in effect, final.

Third, the OPB has a general jurisdiction to supervise the financial solvency of private schemes. We have already looked at this power in Chapter 4. Schemes have to make regular returns of information to the OPB which can, in an extreme case, order an employer to put extra funds into a scheme to ensure its solvency. The board can also monitor the range of investments of a scheme, in particular to stop excessive amounts of money being put into any one investment (*i.e.* to safeguard the scheme in case that investment fails), or into self-investment (*i.e.* investment in the employer's own business).

Fourth, the OPB may give advice to schemes. This is a very necessary function, given the complexity of the laws in this area. It does so principally by publishing memoranda on the various legal aspects of running a pension fund. A list of the current publications is set out in Appendix 2. The Board is in the process of consolidating and republishing some of these memoranda, but this work has been slowed down by financial cut-backs.

Fifth, the OPB may be required to give advice to the Government. Whenever new pensions-related laws are proposed, the OPB scrutinise them first and, if appropriate, make comments and suggestions on them. More widely than that, the OPB may be asked by the Government to investigate particular aspects of pensions and produce reports on them. At the time of writing this book, the OPB were considering remits on solvency, transfers of pension rights and maintenance of the value of preserved benefits.

As stated above, a good overall view of the practical work of the OPB in all of these fields can be gained by study of its annual reports, which are available from HMSO.

7 Member Participation and the Role of Trade Unions in Private Schemes

When we turn to the question of the role that should be played in pension schemes by the people actually contributing to them (and possibly their trade unions), we encounter a problem that is not exactly new—the problem of efficiency versus democracy. This is not to say that the two are completely incompatible but, if there is any truth in the old saying that a camel is a horse designed by a committee, it must be accepted that sometimes the balance can be a difficult one to keep. This is always the case where an organisation needs "lay" participation (for example on a board of directors, board of school governors or university council), but it becomes even more difficult in an area such as pension schemes where the subject matter is so extremely complicated that there is a temptation to leave it all to the experts. Further, it is an area where management could argue that it is not appropriate to have lay representatives on the body that runs the scheme, simply on the ground of the complexity of the decisions that have to be made. It is true that very difficult issues are raised here (and, as we shall see, acute political controversy), but it is fairly clear that simple paternalism on the part of the employer is in most cases no longer an acceptable basis for running a pension scheme (particularly a contributory one), and so the problem of participation has to be faced.

The problem can be split up into two separate but interlinked questions—what information should be given to members and/or their unions, and what measure of control should they have? The Occupational Pensions Board considered this matter in their 1975 Report on "Solvency, Disclosure of Information and Member Participation," which was followed in 1976 by the Labour Government's White Paper on "The Role of Members in the Running of Schemes." However, this produced such controversy, particularly over the question of trade union involvement, that the actual proposals have not, for the most part, been put into law, and under the present Conservative Government there is little likelihood of it happening. We must now look at the main points that arise in this context.

(1) Member participation

Most people involved in the administration of pension schemes would agree that it is necessary in practice to give members of a scheme a certain amount of information about administrative arrangements, benefits and contributions. This is often done by producing booklets for those involved, though immediately problems arise—how can you explain the workings of a very complicated scheme accurately, but in simple language? Once again, it is a question of balance, since the ordinary member would not understand complicated financial information, and yet the employer must avoid producing a booklet that is so simplistic as to be an insult to the members' intelligence (particularly as it concerns a scheme into which they are paying their own money, and which will be vital to them in later life). We shall return shortly to this problem.

Turning to the question of membership participation in the control of the scheme, opinions can become more divided. In its 1975 report, the OPB came down clearly in favour of member participation, having fully considered the arguments against it. They saw in particular the following advantages:

(a) improved staff relations, including a greater feeling of security among members, and the psychological advantages of seeing a partnership working, of having easier access to scheme officials, and of exercising control over their administration of the scheme;

(b) greater appreciation by members of the value of the scheme, particularly the cost involved for the employer and the importance of their own contributions; and

(c) the value of the members' special knowledge in exercising discretionary powers in death benefit cases and in considering cases of hardship.

In addition to this, the report saw three areas where participation would be particularly desirable. First, if there was any question of restricting the investment power of the trustees (*e.g.* a policy of non-investment in a particular country), this could best be done by member representations, since the trustees are simply under a duty to make the best investments, wherever they might be. Second, participation might be generally desirable when deciding on broad questions, such as exercising discretionary powers to increase pension levels, remedying deficiencies in the fund, or appointing or dismissing the scheme's advisers. Third, the OPB considered direct involvement of members advantageous in the general management of the fund, on such questions as making discretionary payments, negotiating transfers to other funds, disclosing information to members, preparing an annual report, and deciding the overall investment policy (though here it must be recognised that in practice much would depend on expert advice given to the trustees).

Given this background of general agreement that *some* information should be provided, and of a certain emphasis towards actual participation in control (at least on the part of the official bodies), we must see what the present law is, and what proposals for change have been made.

(2) Disclosure of information

The present legal position is that, as seen already in Chapter 6, an employer who wishes to establish a scheme must give certain details of it to people who are already employed by him, and must also consult their unions. Once a scheme is established, however, a further (and more important) question arises of what information must be given subsequently (possibly on a regular basis)? The only actual legal requirement here is that, under the contracts of employment legislation (now contained in the Employment Protection (Consolidation) Act 1978, s. 1), a person who is taken on by the employer must be given in writing, notification of certain major terms of employment within 13 weeks of starting the job. These terms include "any terms or conditions relating to . . . pensions and pension schemes," and the employer must also state whether a contracting-out certificate is in force for the employment in question. This is not, however, as important as it sounds, for two reasons: first, it only applies to new employees, and does not lay down what information must be given regularly to all members; second, it is phrased in a vague manner, and the extent of this obligation on the employer has never really been tested (on a narrow view, it could be argued that the employer only has to give notice of the relevant "term or condition," and that may be quite simply that the employee must belong to the pension scheme for the time being in force, and must contribute a certain percentage of his income to it).

At present, therefore, the law does not impose wide-ranging requirements on the employer (certainly once the scheme has been established). The CBI published in June 1973 a booklet entitled "Guidance on provision of information to members of occupational pension schemes," which went some way towards encouraging the divulging of information:

"The information required by [the law] will not, in itself, be enough. Management should ensure that their employees have access to all the relevant information, and, so far as is reasonable and practicable to do so, make provision for this information to be clearly explained. The spirit in which communication of information is undertaken is more important than the precise letter of what is communicated." The booket then went on to suggest four categories of information which ought to be disclosed: (*i*) information which must be given to a new employee under what is now section 1 of the 1978 Act (above); (*ii*) information which should be given to employees on or before joining a pension scheme (in particular, benefits, contributions, financing and administration); (*iii*) information which should be given to members or other beneficiaries when entitlement to benefit arises (in particular, amounts which are payable, and the effects of tax); (*iv*) periodic personal and financial information. This last heading was perhaps the widest, covering requests by individual members for information on their current position in the scheme, and periodic disclosure of the overall financial situation of the scheme (though the "period" in question here was to be "not less than once every five years"; and what was clearly envisaged was information in non-technical language, aimed at the members themselves, not necessarily highly detailed information which might be of use to their unions).

In spite of this guidance, the OPB stated in their 1975 report that they had found the practice of releasing information very variable, with some schemes showing a marked reluctance to disclose anything other than very basic information. This view was supported by the fifth survey of the Government Actuary, 1975 (published 1978), which showed that the only materials consistently made available by a majority of schemes were the detailed rules and the trust deed, which, ironically, were likely to be of least use to the lay reader and did not primarily concern the continued running of the scheme.

In the light of this, the OPB recommended that there should be laws obliging schemes to disclose:

(a) specified financial information, on a regular basis;

this could correspond to the sort of information which should be made available to the OPB itself, and the best way to provide it would probably be an annual report;

(b) certain non-financial information, concerning the scheme and its financing benefits and administration; this should be provided to new members, early leavers, those retiring and other beneficiaries;

(c) individual benefit statements; these should be given to members who make reasonable requests for information on their position;

(d) information on the methods of appointing the management committee of the fund.

The idea was that members would then be at liberty to hand this information over to their unions if they wished to do so. The OPB itself would have powers to make a reluctant scheme disclose these matters.

The Government White Paper of 1976, which followed the OPB report, agreed with these proposals, but they got no further, and so far have not been put into law. It therefore remains for the scheme managers to decide what information to release and how to do it. As we shall see in heading (6) below, it *may* be possible to use the general union rights to disclosure of information in this context, but arguably it would be better if there was definite legal guidance specifically on this point.

(3) Involvement of unions in setting up a scheme

We have already seen in Chapter 6 that the emphasis in the existing law is on involving independent trade unions at the stage of deciding whether to set up a contracted-out scheme, and that they have certain rights to information, and rights to be consulted, which are enforceable by industrial tribunals. The involvement of unions becomes much more contentious, however, when we turn to the possible involvement of unions in the running of schemes, once they have been set up.

(4) Involvement of unions in running a scheme

Three main questions arise when considering member and/or union participation in the control of pension schemes:

(i) Should members be represented?
(ii) If so, how should the law enforce it?
(iii) How should the representation work?

On the first question, the complexity of pension scheme administration could lead to the argument that the vast amounts of assets involved in funded schemes should not be put into the hands of people with little or no understanding of the subject, still less into the hands of external bodies such as trade unions. Such arguments were not accepted by the OPB in their 1975 report. As stated above, they approved the general idea of member participation, but found once again that existing practice was very variable. Likewise, there was a great divergence in the ways in which schemes are administered, leading naturally to a lack of uniformity on participation. The Government Actuary's fifth survey (1975) showed that at that time two-thirds of private schemes had no member representatives, and that of those that did, a clear majority had nominated members, rather than elected members (though it should be noted that these statistics relate to the *number* of schemes, not to the number of *members covered.* When you look at membership figures, the picture changes, for more people are covered by schemes *with* member representation than *without* it, presumably due to representation being more common in the larger schemes. The fact remains, however, that even on these figures nomination of representatives was more common than election).

Turning to the second question—how member participation should be enforced—the OPB and the then Government parted company. The OPB thought that the variety of schemes was so great that it would be very difficult to enforce a uniform pattern of representation. They accepted that 50 per cent. member representation was a worthwhile aim, but recommended that, instead of legislation to enforce it, there should be *(a)* a code of practice on participation, aimed at helping extension of representation by local collective bargaining, and *(b)* an extension of training facilities for the education in pension matters of people likely to become member representatives. Their emphasis was therefore clearly upon voluntary action, partly because at the time this could be viewed as just one aspect of the trend towards "industrial democracy". However, when the 1975 report came to be reviewed in the Government White Paper of 1976, the Government took a stronger view, advocating legislation to give members a right to 50 per cent. representation on schemes' managing bodies. This ran into powerful opposition, particularly from the CBI, and eventually the proposal was dropped. It is probably true to say, however, that the real controversy arose over the third question.

That question is—how should representation work? The proposal in the White Paper was that the right to 50 per cent. representation should belong solely to independent trade unions recognised by the employer in respect of the members concerned. This would have meant a right of appointment by those unions, not a right of election (either by all the members or, alternatively, by those scheme members who were not members of the relevant unions). This proposal should now be seen in its historical context, for at that time there was strong union pressure on the Government for new legal rights to be given to independent trade unions, to the exclusion of lesser associations (such as staff associations or "house" unions) and, arguably, to the exclusion of people who were not union members. This tendency could be seen in the Employment Protection Act 1975 which gave major new legal rights to unions and their members; and in the 1976 Amendment to the Trade Union and Labour Relations Act 1974, which tightened up the law on the closed shop, extended union immunities, and removed the union member's statutory protection from arbitrary or unreasonable exclusion or expulsion from the union. Indeed, this proposal to concentrate pension representation in the hands of independent trade unions has a direct parallel in the law relating to the appointment of safety representatives and safety committees; under the Health and Safety at Work Act 1974, as originally drafted, safety representatives could be *(a)* appointed by recognised trade unions and/or *(b)* elected directly by the employees in question, but in 1975, alternative *(b)* was removed by statute, so that safety representatives can only be union-appointed. In favour of this development, it can of course be argued that *effective* representation in practice can only mean representation by a proper trade union, but it is hardly surprising that it was the main focus for opposition to the last Government's proposals. As the Director-General of the CBI said in 1976:

"But the issue is not only about whether we want trade unions to dominate the way in which the £20,000 million of occupational pension fund money is invested, or about the risks which biased fund management could create for the security of pensioners' money. The question is whether the Government will be allowed to go on and on giving trade unionists rights, while denying them to non-unionised employees."

The position now, therefore, is that the present law does not make schemes have member representatives, and under the present Government it is not likely that any further moves will be made in that direction.

Moreover, the whole movement towards industrial democracy seems to have creaked to a halt, certainly for the time being. However, that is *not* to say that member participation as such is dead. Far from it. In October 1977, the CBI published a booklet entitled "Participation by members in the management of occupational pension schemes—a guide to good practice," which gave clear encouragement for voluntary movement towards member participation (supporting the approach of the OPB), basing their suggestions for future "good practice" on what they said is already standard practice in larger companies, though with considerable variations in detailed arrangements.

(5) The TUC approach

Trade union involvement in pension schemes may take one or both of two quite distinct forms. First, a union may wish to *negotiate* upon the form of a scheme which is to be set up, or upon improvements which it would like to see in an existing scheme (*e.g.* over the levels of contributions which have to be paid by its members). This it can do from the outside, by normal negotiating techniques, and the TUC booklet "Occupational Pension Schemes" (February 1976) gives useful guidance on this function. Second, the union may wish to *participate* in the actual running of the scheme, as we have already seen. Here, there is of course less scope for the promotion of particular interests or factions, because of the restraints upon the office of trustee. These two functions should not be seen as mutually contradictory, though a union involved in a pension scheme may have to keep the distinction between them clearly in mind.

The TUC looked to the last Government for legislation to promote union involvement, particularly with regard to participation. That did not happen, and the TUC has of course accepted that there is now little chance of such legislation under the present Government. However, that does not mean that interest has waned on their part—in fact, quite the opposite. The practical involvement of unions continues to increase, with active TUC encouragement. When the General Secretary, Len Murray, addressed the 1978 Conference of the National Association of Pension Funds (NAPF), he said this:

> "One argument which is often advanced against the additional statutory requirements on pension schemes that are sought by trade unions is that legislation on issues like member representation . . . will discourage

employers from setting up or even maintaining their existing schemes.

This, I believe, repeats the old error of regarding pension schemes as in some ways acts of charity on the part of the employer. This concept is completely rejected by trade unions and, more and more, by employers. It is workpeople who pay for their pension scheme. The money that is set aside to provide them is the property of the workers. The employer's part is to put up the money—just as he does for wages—in return for labour. It will therefore be workpeople, negotiating through their trade unions, who will in large part decide whether pension schemes are established and how they are run . . . .

I remember, 20 years ago, trying to get one of our TUC Committees to take a more active view of unions negotiating pension schemes, and being rapped over the knuckles for what was regarded as an attempt to distract attention from the real job of unions.

Thankfully, that attitude has disappeared, and trade unions now see occupational pension schemes as part of the total package of remuneration which can be provided by an employer. As such, they are an eminently proper subject for collective bargaining. Effective collective bargaining is based both on knowledge and experience, which more and more trade unions are acquiring, and this is reflected, and to some extent initiated, in the TUC itself."

This is a clear statement of the increasing TUC involvement, which is shown by the issuing of the TUC booklet mentioned above (being revised for republication at the time of writing this book), the effort put into training courses for negotiators and pension fund trustees, and the increasing ability of the TUC to assist unions in dealing with individual pension problems.

Later on in his speech, Mr. Murray set out the following general objectives for union negotiators:

(i) The appointment of at least 50 per cent. of the

pension scheme trustees and members of management committees by the independent recognised trade unions that represent scheme members.

(ii) Inflation protection of the preserved benefits of those who have left service prior to retirement and/or the provision of proper facilities for pension transfers on changing job.

(iii) Inflation protection of pension benefits in course of payment so that, during their retirement, pensioners are able on average to maintain the standard of living they achieved at retirement.

(iv) Retirement for men as well as women members from the age of 60, particularly for those who are employed in hazardous or arduous occupations.

(v) Provision for years of back-service by existing employees to count for benefit calculations purposes when a new scheme is introduced or an existing scheme is improved.

(vi) Equal treatment for men and women members with the same benefits paid under the same conditions.

(vii) Provision in an appropriate form of full information on the scheme for members and their independent recognised trade unions.

Given the lack of legislation, the emphasis of the TUC approach is thus clearly upon the use of collective bargaining as a way of altering and improving pension schemes (both as to their organisation, and as to benefits payable under them).

(6) Use of other legal rights by unions

If the present legislation gives no definite legal rights to unions to participate in pension fund management, are there any other legal rights which could be used instead? A union wishing to gain recognition as the proper bargaining agent on pension matters with a particular employer might in the past have used the statutory procedure for gaining recognition (or further recognition, where it is already recognised for other purposes) under the Employment Protection Act 1975. However, following grave legal difficulties in operating this procedure (see, for example, the *Grunwick* case) the whole law on it has been repealed in the Employment Act 1980.

Perhaps a better prospect for a union in the future might be to try to use the provisions in the EPA 1975, ss. 17 to 21, which give independent trade unions rights to receive certain bargaining information. This might fill the gap left by the failure to give a definite statutory right to *pension* information, discussed above. Section 17 requires an employer to release information which is (*a*) "information without which the trade union representatives would be to a material extent impeded in carrying on collective bargaining"; and (*b*) "information which it would be in accordance with good industrial relations practice that the employer should disclose." This vague requirement is made rather more specific by the ACAS Code of Practice No. 2, which expands on the sort of information which, in practice, might come within section 17. The Act then goes on, in section 18, to give certain defences to an employer who does not wish to disclose; so that, for example, the obligation to disclose does not apply if the information in question was given to the employer in confidence, or relates to a particular individual, or would cause substantial injury to the employer's firm if released.

Can a union use this legal right, and the statutory procedure for enforcing it, (see again, Kidner's *Trade Unions*) in order to obtain pension-related information? There is no reason why it should not try. Pension information is not excluded from the range of section 17, and, as we have seen, in modern conditions improvements in pension schemes will probably be regarded as a proper area for collective bargaining. Two notes of caution should be sounded, however. The first is that the ACAS Code of Practice No. 2 does not contain any reference to pension scheme matters when giving guidance on what might have to be disclosed. The OPB suggested in their 1975 report that it should, but this was not done. That is, of course, not fatal to a claim, as the Code is only advisory and is expressly *not* meant to be an exhaustive check-list. However, it would have made matters clearer if there had been some such reference. The second is that some pension information might be of a heavily financial nature, or might fall within the section 18 list of cases where the employer need not disclose. As a generalisation, it is probably easier to claim non-financial information under the section 17 procedure (such as information concerning terms and conditions, manpower planning, training costs and overall pay bills), and so a union must be prepared to make a strong case if it wishes to use the procedure to obtain financial pension information. To take an example, in the case of *Ignall Industries Ltd. and APEX* (CAC Award 79/121), the union requested details of a directors' pension scheme for use in negotiations on a staff scheme. When the employer refused to release such details, the union tried to obtain them under the legal procedure, but the CAC dismissed their claim on two grounds: (i) the union had not shown that they were in fact "materially impeded in collective bargaining" without the information; and (ii) in any event, this information was saved from disclosure by one of the exceptions in section 18 since it could relate to particular individuals. It should be noted, however, that this case does *not* say that pension matters are outside the scope of section 17, and so it is open to a union to try to use the legal procedure for gaining such information, though this case shows that they should approach such a claim with care and thought, since the procedure, as drafted, has several traps for the unwary.

(7) Training in pension matters

It should be clear that the general movement (in practice, if not yet in law) is towards member participation. That fact does not, however, alter the fact that pension scheme management is an extremely complicated subject. That fact is no longer widely seen as necessarily an argument *against* having participation, but it does mean that training in pension matters must be seen as an essential part of such participation. The OPB in its 1975 report certainly thought so, and recommended more in-house training by employers.

Much of the initiative here has in fact come from the union movement, both at TUC and individual union level. Seminars or whole courses on pensions are not uncommon at union training establishments, and they aim to instruct people who are likely to come into contact with pension schemes at both the negotiating and management levels (*i.e.* those who are going to be negotiating with the employer from the outside on benefits, etc., under the scheme, and those who may be involved from the inside as member representative trustees). The TUC has always been rather suspicious of any courses put on by outside bodies, over which it does not have control; but there is no reason why union courses should not at least draw on outside expertise, for example from the Company Pensions Information Centre (CPIC—see Appendices 1 and 2), which exists partly to provide speakers, seminars and courses for any interested organisations.

One final point to notice here is that unions wishing to run such courses, or co-ordinate their activities in the pensions sphere (for example with other unions), may be able once again to take advantage of the general law on industrial relations. The law which may be particularly important here is to be found in the Employment Protection Consolidation Act 1978, ss. 27 to 32, which gives rights to:

(*a*) paid time off work for union officials to carry out certain union duties or relevant training in aspects of industrial relations; and

(*b*) unpaid time off work for union members for the purposes of certain trade union activities.

This is a complicated matter; the bare statutory provisions are supplemented by the ACAS Code of Practice No. 3, "Time off for trade union duties and activities," and the topic is covered in detail in Gillian Morris's book in this series, *Union Members*. For present purposes, it is enough to say that these rights, particularly (*a*) above, could be important to help union officials to take a full part in pension negotiations and administration. In a case called

Young v. *Carr Fasteners Ltd.*, 1979, Mrs. Young was a GMWU shop steward who attended a union-approved course on "Pensions and Participation" at Woodstock College. Her employer refused to pay her for the time off. The problem was that her employer's pension scheme was established *without* member trustees (being run by an insurance company, with three director trustees), and there were no immediate plans to include any. Because of that, the industrial tribunal, when asked by Mrs. Young to order the employer to pay her for the time off, refused to do so on the ground that, as there was no participation in the scheme, the training in question was not relevant to any *existing* industrial relations matters, and so did not come within the statutory right. When Mrs. Young appealed against this, the Employment Appeal Tribunal held in her favour and reversed the tribunal's decision. They said that the tribunal had taken too narrow a view on what could be a relevant industrial relations matter, and went on to say this:

> "It seems clear to us that negotiations about pension rights, and advising members about pension rights are as much a part of industrial relations as negotiating and advising about wage levels. We do not consider that the fact that the scheme was administered in such a way that no further employee could at the moment be made a trustee, or that the scheme was substantially administered in accordance with the advice of the insurance company, is conclusive . . . . It seems to us that the company's employees may need advice as to their participation in the company's pension scheme. Moreover, employees may well wish to consider making representations to the company as to changes in the structure or administration of the scheme . . . . Accordingly, instruction on member participation in pension schemes as covered by this course constituted 'training in aspects of industrial relations relevant to the carrying out of the duties of a trade union official.' "

This case demonstrates the importance of the modern

practical approach of regarding pensions as stored-up financial rights for the individual employees, and therefore as a proper subject of collective bargaining and industrial relations. Training is just one aspect of this, but one which should not be underestimated.

8 Preservation of Pension Rights for Early Leavers

The problem

Pension rights are built up over the years of employment, and so continuity of employment is an important factor. When an employee stays in the same employment (or only moves around within one organisation or group), he or she may occasionally look up the pension rights, for example in the pension scheme booklet, and look forward to them continuing to increase with both the passing of the years and continued promotion to higher paid positions. This is the way in which we normally think of a typical pension scheme operating.

As in any area of law, however, the rules have to take account of *un*typical cases. One particular problem which has arisen in the area of pensions concerns what is to happen to an "early leaver." If someone leaves the employment in question before (and possibly *well* before) the retirement age, what is to happen to his stored up pension rights? This becomes particularly crucial in the case of someone who changes employment several times in the course of his or her working life.

There are four main ways in which the problem may be solved:

(i) Contributions refund. The employee takes back from the fund the amount that he has paid in.

(ii) Preservation of pension rights. The employee has his entitlement "frozen" within the scheme, so that when he eventually reaches pension age he receives a part-pension from that scheme (based on his years of service with that employer) in addition to other pension payments from his later employer or employers.

(iii) Transfer. If his new employer runs a pension scheme, it may be possible for him to have his existing entitlement with scheme A transferred to scheme B and to keep on contributing while working for that new employer.

(iv) State scheme. He will remain entitled to the basic State pension whatever happens. Now that the State scheme has been improved by the additional element, it *may* be possible for him to "buy his way back into" the full State scheme and so rely on that instead of any further occupational scheme.

Until the 1970s, the employee usually did not have this range of choice. Normally when an employee left pensioned employment he had to take a refund of his contributions. In theory, he could invest this wisely to secure future benefits in other ways, but in practice of course the temptation to spend it might be strong (particularly if, for example, the change of job entailed an expensive move of house). Moreover, he would usually lose out anyway, since he would only get back his own contributions—he could not withdraw the employer's contributions principally because this is not allowed by the Inland Revenue—and so the total value of the refund would be less than the continuing stored-up value if he had stayed with the same employer. Preservation and transfers were always legally possible, but in 1971 the Government Actuary's survey of pension funds found that less than one in ten leavers in fact had one of these options open to them. Further, the survey found that the position was not improving by itself. The cash refund was the common answer, and was arguably a major weakness of the law on occupational pension schemes. The lack of preservation or transfers may have encouraged long and stable service with one employer, but it could also act harshly (for example, putting valuable pension rights at risk if there was a possibility of the employee being sacked).

In the light of this, a lot of effort has been put into changing the legal rules to lessen the need to take cash refunds, and to encourage preservation and, to a lesser extent, transfer of pension rights when changing jobs.

Preservation—the new rules

Legislation in 1973 gave pension scheme employees an important new right. Once a member was over 26, and had worked for the employer for five years, he became *entitled* to a preserved ("frozen") pension if he later left that employment. Schemes had to provide for this, and this is now a condition for contracting out. That only went half way. The full scheme, as it now applies, is that once a member has met those qualifications, he now *cannot* take a refund of his contributions if he leaves employment (at least to the extent that those contributions were made after April 1975); his entitlement (called now "short term benefits") must be preserved in some way.

Preservation is therefore the modern answer to the problem of the early leaver, and the OPB is there to enforce the new scheme. Normally preservation will be achieved within the pension fund or by the purchasing of an annuity. Complicated laws surround the preservation rules, aimed at ensuring that people with short service benefits (*i.e.* those who have left the employment) are not treated less favourably than those still in employment and contributing into the fund. In particular, that part of the preserved benefits which represents the guaranteed minimum pension (GMP) must be increased to take account of inflation, though the pension fund is given a choice of ways of achieving this.

One practical problem relating to preservation, on which the law is silent, is that if the frozen pension is to be paid when the early leaver eventually reaches retirement age, the pension fund managers must be able to *find* that person. The keeping of records will therefore become very important, and it will clearly be in the early leaver's interests to make sure that the pension fund knows of his whereabouts when he retires. In the case of a person who changes job several times, this could become complicated, and is a factor for him to bear in mind.

There are two important alternatives to the frozen pension when someone leaves employment. The first is that when an employee leaves before having served for five years, the employer may "buy him back into" the full State pension scheme by paying to the State out of the pension fund a "contributions equivalent premium" which puts the employee back into the same position as if he had been paying into the State scheme all of the time. Second, where the employee *has* served for five years and so is covered by the preservation rules, it may be possible to safeguard his pension entitlement by *transferring* it to a new scheme (where his new employer also maintains such a contracted-out scheme). This will then operate instead of a frozen pension. Where there is a scheme attached to the new employment, this may seem the logical choice, *but* it may not be as simple as it at first seems. The problem is that most private schemes differ, and certainly are run independently of each other. This may mean that there has to be a process of bargaining between the old and new schemes (probably in practice between their actuaries) to reach terms on which the new scheme will give credit of sorts for past employment in return for a transfer of funds from the old scheme. One problem (certainly where the idea is for the new scheme to add notional years of employment on to the employee's actual period of employment with the new employer) is that those years will cost more and more for the new scheme to finance as the employee's salary increases (since the eventual pension will be based on his final salary or final average salary), although of course the new employer in fact did not have the beneft of his work during those years. Public sector pension schemes tend to be so similar that an employee moving from one public employer to another may be able to count the whole of his service with the old employer when claiming a pension from the new employer (through the so-called "transfer club" in the public sector). This is much less likely to be the case in the private sector, where the new employer is likely to require a "discount" (*i.e.* to give credit for fewer years than the employee in fact worked for the old employer, in return for agreeing to the transfer). However, if the employee's salary from the new employer is likely to increase steadily, he may in practice soon make up for that deficiency.

Even from the discussion so far, it can be seen that the question of transfer (especially where the early leaver has to decide whether to take a frozen pension *or* a particular transfer that is on offer) can be an extremely complicated one, and all that can be said here is that if an employee is faced with this sort of decision he ought to seek specialist expert advice before coming to a decision.

One final point to notice on the preservation rules is that they are not restricted to employees who leave of their own accord. They also apply to employees who are sacked, whether for redundancy, misconduct, inefficiency or any other reason. Thus, loss of pension rights is no longer a stick to hold over employees who work badly or threaten to go on strike, for example. It is true that the legislation does allow accrued pension rights to be suspended or forfeited in certain circumstances, but these are not likely to apply to the majority of pensioners, as they apply to such cases as insanity, treason and contravention of certain sections of the Official Secrets Act.

The practical position on changing jobs

The position of the employee who changes employment, possibly several times, in the course of his working life is better than it was because of the new preservation rules, and he or she is less likely to end up just with a flat-rate State pension plus a minimal pension from the last employer. Also, although the full preservation scheme is now in operation, that is not the end of the matter, as the OPB have been requested by the Government to inquire further into the subject to see if further improvements can be made in the areas of transfers between schemes and the maintenance of the value of frozen benefits.

However, in most cases a person who changes employment can expect to suffer *some* loss of pension position, even if only temporarily. At certain times in life, this may seem a negligible disadvantage compared with the advantages of a move (for example where prospects in the new job are much better), and the employee may confidently expect to make up the difference sooner rather than later. At other times in life (for example when approaching pension age or at a time of static prospects), the effects of a move on his pension position could be a significant factor which the employee ought to consider fully. The reasons for the loss are quite straightforward. In the case of a frozen pension, the eventual calculation of that part of his pension will be based on his salary at the time of the move, not on his final salary at the time of retirement, which may make a significant difference, even after taking into account the legal requirements of a certain amount of inflation-proofing of preserved benefits. In the case of a transfer, the employee may only be credited with a "discounted" level of past service, for the reasons discussed above.

Once again, the only sound advice that can be given is that if the employee thinks that his pension position might be significantly jeopardised, he should seek professional advice before deciding whether or not to move. One principal factor in making the decision will be how much higher the salary for the new job will be, since part of that will, in effect, have to go towards making up for the damage to his pension position done by the move. How variable the position might be can be seen from the table printed below. It was prepared and published in 1980 by Tom Shucksmith of Shucksmith & Co., Consulting Actuaries, of Reigate, Surrey, to whom the author of this book is indebted for permission to reproduce it. The table is not meant to be the final word on the subject for all cases and schemes, since it is based on certain interest rate and earning assumptions and reflects what its author calls a "representative good pension scheme: normal retirement age is 65; benefits are 1/60th of final average salary for each year's service; widows pension of 50 per cent both before and after retirement; and death cover of twice salary; post-retirement pension increases of 3 per cent; members contribution rate of 5 per cent." It gives in columns 3 and 4 a fascinating insight into the practical effects of a change of employment on pension position, particularly for employees aged over about 45, or with more than 10 years' service:

PAY RISE NEEDED TO RESTORE LOSS OF PENSION POSITION

(1) Age of man at withdrawal	(2) Pensionable service completed at withdrawal	(3) Value of loss of pension position per £10,000 pa salary	(4) Salary increase (as percentage of old salary) to compensate for (3)
30	5	5,250	1½
35	5	5,250	2
	10	11,500	4
40	5	5,500	2
	10	11,750	4½
	15	17,500	7
45	5	5,500	3
	10	11,000	5½
	15	16,500	8
	20	22,000	11
50	5	5,000	3½
	10	10,000	6½
	15	15,000	10
	20	20,000	13
	25	25,000	17
55	5	4,250	4
	10	8,250	8
	15	12,500	12
	20	16,500	16
	25	20,750	20
	30	25,000	24
60	5	2,750	5
	10	5,500	10
	15	8,250	16
	20	11,000	21
	25	13,750	26
	30	16,500	32
	35	19,500	37

9 Equal Access for Women and the Effect of Anti-Discrimination Laws

The questions of whether women should receive the same pension treatment as men, and if so how it should be done, immediately raise problems of an historical and actuarial nature. The main problem is that it has been well established for many years in this country that women retire earlier than men; and actuarial problems arise from the fact that women tend to live longer than men, work for less years during a career (particularly if they have children), and tend to stay for shorter periods with one employer (particularly when younger). Thus, there are strong pressures for *un*equal treatment of women. Even the apparently attractive requirement of "equal pensions for equal contributions" can be argued to be unfair, since in the real world an actuary might be able to show that this would mean the same pension as a man for a longer retirement period (since women live longer) in return for the same contributions as a man but paid over a shorter working life.

However, the modern tendency in the law is towards the eradication of sex-based differences. We now have the Equal Pay Act 1970 and the Sex Discrimination Act 1975, with the Equal Opportunities Commission (EOC) established to promote sexual equality by a variety of activities and legal powers. We now have to see how these developments affect pensions. As stated above, there are strong practical objections to equality in this field, but on the other hand, it can be argued that it is exactly in fields such as this that equality is such an important aim, since more and more women are working for more and more of their working lives, and pensions are just as much a part of their pay and conditions as they are for male employees. It has been estimated recently that 66 per cent. of married women have jobs, and the Government Actuary's 1975 survey showed that of the 11.5 million employees who were members of occupational pension schemes, 2.8 million were women. If anything, these proportions are likely to grow. In the light of this, the legal developments have been, at best, cautious. Further reforms have been suggested, but as yet have not proceeded very far. One major source of information here is the OPB's 1976 report on "Equal status for men and women in occupational pension schemes" (Cmnd. 6599). One interesting possibility, as we shall see, is that the present United Kingdom position might be outflanked by EEC laws on equal pay. First, however, we must look at the existing law.

Anti-discrimination laws and pensions

Legal moves towards sex equality led to the passing of the Equal Pay Act 1970 and the Sex Discrimination Act 1975. The former requires that women shall receive equal pay and conditions for equal work, and the latter applies to employment matters outside pay and conditions, such as selection, advertising of jobs, promotion and dismissal. Together they are aimed at covering all the most significant aspects of employment. However, pensions are an exception to that.

Both Acts (as originally drafted) contain subsections which exclude from the operation of their anti-discrimination rules "provisions in relation to death or retirement." This means that, as far as those Acts are concerned, pension schemes may legally make separate and/or discriminatory provisions for men or women. This is a very wide exclusion, as can be seen from the judgments of the Court of Appeal in two out of three leading cases (the third is considered separately below) which were heard together. In the first, *Garland* v. *British Rail Engineering Ltd.*, 1979, Mrs. Garland complained under the Sex Discrimination Act 1975 about a practice by British Rail that when employees retired, male pensioners got travel concessions for themselves and their families, but female pensioners only got similar concessions for themselves. In the second case, *Turton* v. *MacGregor Wallcoverings Ltd.*, 1979, Mrs. Turton complained under the same Act about a redundancy scheme which gave increased benefits to employees made redundant when over 60, her complaint being that women had to retire at 60 and so could not qualify for the better redundancy rights. In both cases, the Court of Appeal held that the Act could not apply, since both practices were "provisions in relation to death or retirement," and so were not illegal.

Equal access

Given that the normal anti-discrimination laws are ineffective in the pensions field, what is to be done to safeguard women in schemes? The cautious answer so far has been to provide a legal right to what is called "equal access." As from April 1978, a woman has had a right to equality of *access* to a pension scheme (this is contained in the Social Security Pensions Act 1975 and a set of specialised regulations). This means that a scheme must be open to both men and women on terms which are the same as to *(a)* the age and length of service needed to become a member, and *(b)* whether membership is voluntary or obligatory.

A pension scheme must conform to this equal access requirement if it is to be allowed to contract out, and the OPB is there to give help in problem cases. The law goes beyond simple help, however. If a person who is or wishes to be a member of a scheme thinks that the equal access requirement is not being observed, she may do one of two things:

(a) she may complain to the OPB, which has powers to investigate, make a ruling, and force a scheme to comply with the law; *or*

(b) she may complain directly to an industrial tribunal. This is because the Equal Pay Act 1970 has now been slightly amended so that it can be used to enforce pension equality (but only to the extent covered by the equal access requirement). If she takes this course of action, the tribunal may, if it finds in her favour, order modification of the scheme *and* order it to admit her as a member, with back-membership of up to two years. This back-membership must be fully funded by the employer without any contributions by the woman or by the fund itself. This is in place of the normal power of the tribunal under the 1970 Act to award damages.

The law therefore gives fairly full coverage of enforcement provisions, but it is certainly arguable that the *content* of "equal access" does not go far enough. In essence, it only outlaws any discrimination in rules relating to *entry* into a scheme. It does not cover the question of what benefits the woman must have under the scheme (and neither does the Equal Pay Act, for the reasons set out above), so discrimination in benefits is not outlawed (for example, a scheme giving no survivors' benefits to women members). Moreover, discrimination on the basis of marital status might still be lawful. Also, women might be at a significant practical disadvantage too in that in some industries they tend to be in lower paid and/or part-time jobs, and it may be that pension schemes are not established covering that sort of job, with the result that in practice the majority of the women are indirectly excluded from schemes—not because they are women, but because they (more than men) are in jobs outside pension coverage. In other areas, this sort of "indirect discrimination" could be unlawful under the Sex Discrimination Act but, as we have seen, that Act does not apply to pensions.

Thus, equal access goes only so far. The OPB have suggested further reforms, aimed particularly at securing equality of benefits, but it remains an open question as to whether anything more will be done in the foreseeable future.

Two further points might be noticed. The first is that there are no special provisions for women to be trustees of pension schemes, even where large numbers of women are involved. This has been said by some to be desirable, on the basis that women should be represented on the governing bodies, but the OPB considered it and thought it unnecessary. The second point is that women who take their statutory entitlement to maternity leave have their continuity of employment safeguarded for pension purposes. though the time off does not *count* towards pension entitlement. However, that only applies to the limited period of maternity leave laid down by the EPCA 1978. It does not help a woman who takes a longer period off (possible a few years) to raise a family before returning to her work. Perhaps this might be a fruitful area for reform.

The retirement age

The different retirement ages lie at the root of many of the problems relating to women and pensions, since most schemes adopt the State scheme's approach of having a retirement age of 65 for men and 60 for women. In a case called *Roberts* v. *Cleveland Area Health Authority* (the third of the three cases mentioned above), an attempt was made to have a contractual provision that men retire at 65 and women at 60 declared unlawful under the Sex Discrimination Act. The Court of Appeal once again gave a wide interpretation to the exclusion in the Act for "provisions in relation to death or retirement," and held that differing retirement ages remain entirely lawful.

What can be done about such differences? The answer in practice is probably very little. This distinction has long been at the basis of State pensions. (It can also be seen in other areas of employment law. For example, a man can no longer claim unfair dismissal if he is dismissed when over 65, but for a woman the figure is 60, unless there is some other figure specified in her contract.) The Equal

Opportunities Commission are strongly in favour of equalising the pension age, if necessary by increasing the woman's pension age as well as lowering that for men (*e.g.* 63 for all). Indeed, it can be argued that women should be allowed to work longer, to enable them to improve their pension position over their last few years. However, the TUC have taken issue with the EOC on this, and so the union approach may be that any equalisation must be done solely by decreasing the male retirement age. In this area, however, it is important to bear in mind realities. As long ago as 1976, it was estimated that the cost of equalising retirement ages by reducing the male retirement age to 60 would be £2,000 million. In times of financial stringency, this is hardly likely to be a priority. In the meantime, however, some progress might be made on a piecemeal basis towards more flexible retirement ages for both sexes, and early retirement in certain industries, particularly in hazardous or difficult employments such as mining.

(4) Equality in pensions—the EEC dimension

It is sometimes easy to forget that in this country we are now subject to two systems of law—our own and that of the EEC. Article 119 of the Treaty of Rome (which set up the EEC) states that all Member States shall secure the principle of equal pay for equal work. Indeed, the Equal Pay Act 1970 was passed partly to ensure this. However, there is a complicating factor.

This is that Article 119 has been declared by the European Court to be what is called "directly applicable." This means that individuals in Member States can rely on it directly, as giving them definite rights which they may enforce in their own courts. The position therefore seems to be that a woman in the UK who is not being given equal pay can complain to a tribunal *either* under the Equal Pay Act *or* under Article 119. In most cases this will amount to the same thing; but there are certain ways in which the law as set out in the Act may be narrower than that in the Article, in which case the woman might stand to gain by relying on the Article instead. Pension matters may be one such example.

Put briefly, the Article does *not* exclude pensions from its operation, as we have seen that the Act does. It is true that the Article does not expressly include them either; indeed, the main problem with the Article is that it is so vaguely drafted, so that almost everything will depend on the European Court's interpretation of it. At the time of writing this book, the Court of Appeal had referred a pensions case to the European Court for a decision on this point, but no decision had yet been reached. The case is called *Worringham* v. *Lloyds Bank* and concerns Lloyds Bank's pension schemes for men and women. When over 25 and on equal work, the two are treated the same; but under 25, men receive 5 per cent. more salary, this then being taken back as pension contributions, the women's scheme being non-contributory until the age of 25. The reason for this difference is said to be that women tend to leave employment more often than men up to that age. The scheme could however produce inequalities (*e.g.* if a man resigns at 25 he can withdraw his contributions, whereas a women has no such contributions to withdraw), and the EOC supported a challenge to the lawfulness of this particular scheme.

The Court of Appeal said once more that this clearly came within the exemption from the Equal Pay Act of "provisions related to death or retirement," and so the scheme was lawful under English law. However, the Court then went on to consider EEC law, and thought that it was certainly arguable that the scheme might be unlawful under Article 119, and considered it a proper case to send up to the European Court for its authoritative decision. If that Court decides that the Article *does* apply to occupational pension schemes, it could have major repercussions for any pension scheme that makes different arrangements for men and women, and could bring about reforms more quickly than any proposed legislation is likely to do.

10 Protection of Pension Rights on Dismissal and on the Employer's Insolvency

Dismissal of the employee

It used to be the case that if an employee was dismissed he could lose out heavily because of the effects on his pension position. This was particularly so in the days before (a) the present laws on preservation of pension rights (see Chap. 8), and (b) the present remedies before a tribunal for a person who is unfairly dismissed. Because of the preservation rules, the dismissed employee is not now restricted to taking a refund on his own contributions, and may retain his stored up pension rights in a "frozen" condition until his eventual retirement, even if he was sacked for fraud, misconduct or inefficiency. Under a contracted-out scheme, a pension can only be forfeited in highly unusual situations.

In modern conditions, therefore, the actual loss of pension position on dismissal is likely to be less than in the past, although we have seen that people can still suffer quantifiable losses when changing jobs voluntarily. Employees who are fairly sacked also have to put up with some degree of loss; but where an employee is sacked *unfairly*, the law now gives him or her a range of new and more efficient remedies before a tribunal. (On unfair dismissal generally, see Robert Upex's book, *Dismissal*, in this series.) This means that that employee may be able to get compensation which may include an amount for loss of pension rights. So it is most important to be able to calculate the actual loss for the purpose of an unfair dismissal action.

If an ex-employee is found by a tribunal to have been unfairly dismissed, he can in theory claim to be reinstated, *i.e.* put back into his old job. If this happens, his pension position is unaffected, since he is treated as if he had never been sacked. Statistics show, however, that in practice a successful applicant is unlikely to be given the remedy of reinstatement. In 1978, 11,828 cases of unfair dismissal were heard by tribunals; of these, the applicant employee was successful in only 3,277, and only 106 of the successful claims ended in reinstatement. The remedy is therefore more likely to be an award of compensation. This is split into two: the basic award (calculated mathematically on age and length of service, like a redundancy payment), and the compensatory award. The latter is at the tribunal's discretion (though there is a maximum amount, set at £6,250 at the time of writing this book, subject to annual increases), and is meant to be calculated as a realistic estimate of what the employee has actually lost because of being dismissed.

When calculating the compensatory award, it is well established that loss of pension position is one of the matters to be assessed by the tribunal. Beyond that, however, it becomes much more difficult. The calculations that have to be done become extremely complicated, partly because the facts of different cases (and the different pension schemes involved) can vary so much. The sacked employee may go from pensioned employment to non-pensioned employment, from a contributory to a non-contributory scheme, from a better scheme to a worse scheme (or vice versa), or from pensioned employment to the dole. There used to be the further complication that the dismissed employee might have a range of options, including refund of contributions, but with the new preservation laws this at least becomes less of a problem as most early leavers will have to take a frozen pension or a transfer. In the face of all of these complications, the tribunals and the courts have yet to evolve any definite system of assessing pension loss.

Sometimes the view has been expressed by them that a rounded figure should be arrived at by a non-technical and common sense approach. However, this is simply not possible. There has to be *some* proper actuarial basis for the calculation, and the applicant employee (or his legal advisers) should bear in mind the rule that the burden of proof on pension loss lies upon him. So he must arrive at the tribunal with all available evidence on this matter, or the tribunal might take the easy way out and say that, since no evidence was produced, nothing can be awarded.

What rules have been evolved so far by the tribunals and courts are complicated and still only partially developed, though likely to evolve further over the next few years. The basis of them is a split up of the loss into *(a)* loss of present pension position, and *(b)* loss of future pension opportunity (*i.e.* the opportunity, if he had not been dismissed, to improve his pension position by further years of service with that employer). The immediate loss through being dismissed must be set off against any benefits from any other pension scheme which he may join in new employment.

In an attempt to introduce some order into this area, the Government Actuary produced a report in 1980 giving guidance to industrial tribunals on possible methods of assessing pension loss. Once again this is of some complexity, and has not gone unchallenged in the actuarial profession, but one of its main conclusions is that just taking as a yardstick the contributions paid in, and those that would have been paid in had the employee not been dismissed, is too crude a method for most cases. The Government Actuary's Department recommends instead what is called the "actuarial method," which takes more factors into account, some of which relate to future possibilities and contingencies.

The simple message from all of this is that, in any case where loss of pension position is likely to be an important factor, the dismissed employee may be well advised to invest in a consulting actuary's advice. Such a person (or someone else well versed in pension matters) should be able to put a definite figure on the expected loss. Although this is not binding on the tribunal, the employee applicant would at least be going to the hearing prepared, and ready to discharge his burden of proof. Moreover, he may be surprised at the figure which is arrived at, for in some circumstances (to take but one example, a relatively young man with good career prospects) the figure in question may be in thousands rather than hundreds of pounds. In the light of this, it is surprising how low most overall tribunal awards are: In 1978, the median award was £375, with only 17 per cent. of awards being over £1,000, and only 2·5 per cent. over £3,000. Perhaps this is partly because the full potential of loss of pension claims has not been realised, either by applicants or their advisers.

Insolvency of the employer

If the employer becomes insolvent (or "bankrupt"), there is at least the consolation that the pension fund is established as a trust entirely separately, and so the fund itself is not necessarily insolvent. However, in the realities of the situation, it may well be that the employer is the biggest contributor, and may have gone bankrupt owing money in contributions to the fund. In such circumstances, the law gives limited protection in two ways.

First, the fund is given what is called "priority" in the bankruptcy, which means that it has some preference over certain other creditors of the bankrupt employer as to who should be paid first. Thus, up to 12 months' back-contributions to the fund may be claimed as a priority debt. Secondly, the Employment Protection (Consolidation) Act 1978, s. 123, gives a limited guarantee in addition. It provides that any unpaid contributions for the last 12 months before the insolvency may be paid into the pension fund by the Secretary of State for Employment out of the Redundancy Fund. It is then up to the Secretary of State to try to recover this money (or part of it) from the bankrupt employer. If the Secretary of State refuses to pay this money into the pension fund, the fund's administrators may go to a tribunal seeking a ruling that he should do so.

11 Conclusion

We have seen that the complexity of the law and practices surrounding occupational pension schemes can hardly be over-emphasised. The modern movement is towards member involvement, though at varying levels, and it is therefore important that each individual scheme member should have some idea of his or her entitlements and of the workings of the scheme. This may be particularly important if, for example, he or she is thinking of changing jobs or taking early retirement.

Fortunately, the overall framework of pensions in this country is no longer politically controversial, and so we should be able to look forward to the necessary period of stability in order for the system to become fully settled (subject, of course, to the continuing problems caused by inflation). Moreover, the initial period of intense activity due to the coming into force of the new schemes on State pensions and the contracting-out procedure is now over. However, a period of stability is not necessarily going to be one of inactivity. At the time of writing this book, three potential developments are of interest.

The first is that the OPB still has much work in front of it. In particular, it is investigating the major questions of ensuring the solvency of schemes, transfers between schemes, and further developments on maintaining the value of preserved pensions. This may in time lead to further legislation. The second is that the National Association of Pension Funds held an important annual conference in May 1980 at which it adopted a Code of Practice on the information that ought to be given to members of schemes. This shows a new approach, namely, a *voluntary* effort on the part of those involved in administration of pension schemes, possibly as an alternative to further legislation. Thirdly, the committee making a general study of the financial institutions of this country under the chairmanship of Sir Harold Wilson is due to make its report, which is bound to contain a lot of material on pension funds. It may also contain recommendations for more laws governing the control and investment of such funds in the public interest, as well as the interests of members. Some of these may be controversial: for example, it may contain trade union suggestions that a certain percentage of pension fund assets should be directed by the State into industrial investment.

These sorts of controversies are perhaps inevitable now that pension funds are such a major financial force, and it can be predicted with some confidence that, although the overall structure of pension schemes is now well established, there will still be considerable future activity in this area.

Useful Addresses

Occupational Pensions Board/Inland Revenue Superannuation Funds Office, Apex Tower, High Street, New Malden, Surrey KT3 4DN.

Department of Health and Social Security (Occupational Pensions Inquiries), Alexander Fleming House, Elephant and Castle, London, SE1.

National Association of Pension Funds, Prudential House, Wellesley Road, Croydon, Surrey CR0 2AD.

Company Pensions Information Centre, 7 Old Park Lane, London, W1.

Equal Opportunities Commission, Overseas House, Quay Street, Manchester M3 3HN.

Trades Union Congress, Great Russell Street, London, WC1B 3LS

Confederation of British Industry, 21 Tothill Street, London, SW1H 9LP.

Her Majesty's Stationery Office, 49 High Holborn, London, WC1V 6HB.

Relevant Organisations and their Publications

1. The Occupational Pensions Board

The composition and powers of the OPB have already been considered in Chapter 6. In addition to its detailed powers and work, it also publishes documents of guidance. These include the general introductory leaflet OPB1 (being rewritten at the time that this book was written), and three Notes for Guidance:

OP16 Preservation of pensions
OP23 Equal access
OP25 Review of a determination

The OPB is under a legal duty to make an annual report to the Secretary of State for Social Services; these reports contain much useful information, and can be obtained from HMSO.

In addition, the OPB publishes detailed Memoranda; these are not generally available on request, being restricted to a definite mailing list, which was severely pruned several years ago. However, people involved in pension fund administration should be able to find a particular memorandum in which they are interested through a consulting actuary, life office or pensions adviser.

The following Memoranda have been issued by the OPB, some (marked [1]) jointly with the SFO.

No. 18 Preservation of Occupational Pension Rights October 1974

No. 19 Transfer of Pension Rights Between the United Kingdom and the European Communities October 1974

No. 22 Interaction of Preservation Requirements and Conditions for Tax Approval, and Miscelleous Matters June 1975

No. 23 Assistance to Occupational Pension Schemes in Modification or Winding-up August 1975

No. 24 Preservation: Individual Arrangements August 1975

No. 29 Contracting-out: Requirements to be met by Contracted-out Schemes March 1976

No. 30 Contracting-out: Election Procedure March 1976

No. 32 Equal Access to Occupational Pension Schemes for Men and Women April 1976

No. 33 Application of Preservation Requirements to Schemes with an Overseas Element and Transfer of Benefit Rights to Overseas Schemes April 1976

[1]No. 34 Preservation of Occupational Pension Rights 1976 Amending Regulations; Lump Sum and Commutation May 1976

[1]No. 38 Revised Arrangements for the Distribution of Joint Office Memoranda OPB Examination of Documents Submitted to the Joint Office November 1976

No. 40 Contracting-out: Supplementary Requirements; Minor Changes in SFO Practice March 1977

No. 42 Contracting-out: Supplementary Requirements July 1977

No. 43 Contracting-out: Supervision of Scheme Resources by the Occupational Pensions Board July 1977

[1]No. 44 Contracting-out: Interim documentation July 1977

No. 45 Preservation Amendment Regulations 1977: Maternity Absences; Deductions from Benefit, Including Deductions to Take Account of State Scheme Benefits July 1977

No. 50 Interim Documentation January 1978

No. 51 Contracting-out: Part I—Contracted-out Employment (Miscellaneous Provisions) Regulations 1978

Part II—State Scheme Premiums (Actuarial Tables)

Regulations 1978 March 1978

[1]No. 53 Contracting-out: Average Annual Salary Schemes—Commutation of Trivial Pensions May 1978

No. 55 Contracting-out: Part I—Consent of the Occupational Pensions Board to Changes in Scheme Rules

No. 55 Part II—Transfer of Accrued Rights Without the Member's Consent between Contracted-out Schemes August 1978

No. 56 Contracting-out: Supervision of Resources of Self-Administered Schemes Completion of Annual Statement September 1978

[1]No. 61 Preservation and contracting-out Part I—Refunds of Contributions to Early Leavers

[1]No. 61 Part II—Transfer of Pension Rights Between the United Kingdom and the Isle of Man

[1]No. 61 Part III—Revaluation of Transferred Guaranteed Minimum Pensions

[1]No. 61 Part IV—Married Women and Widow Optants

[1]No. 61 Part V—Definitive Documentation and Rule Changes June 1979

No. 62 Contracting-out: Supervision of Scheme Resources Part I—Short Term and Replacement Actuarial Certificates

No. 62 Part II—Modification of Solvency Tests on Provide for Open Market Annuities

No. 62 Part III—Limited Revaluation Schemes using the Alternative Solvency Test

No. 66 Contracting-out: Procedure

2. The DHSS

The DHSS is principally involved with the running of the *State* pension scheme, but of course has to concern itself with the overlap between that scheme and private occupational schemes. With that in mind, it issues the following leaflets (which may be obtained from local DHSS offices):

NP23 Guide for employers: occupational pension schemes (April 1979)

NP29 Guide to procedures on termination of contracted-out employment and related matters (October 1978)

NP32 Your retirement pension (November 1978)

NP34 New pensions: a more secure future (January 1978)

Multiple copies of leaflets may be obtained from the DHSS (Leaflets), P.O. Box 21, Stanmore, Middlesex HA7 1AY.

3. The Government Actuary's Department

The GAD has the responsibility of doing surveys every few years of the size, working, organisation, etc., of private schemes. The last such survey was done in 1975, and the results are published in "Occupational Pension schemes 1975: Fifth Survey of the Government Actuary." It was published in 1978 and is available from HMSO (£2.75).

4. The National Association of Pension Funds

The NAPF was founded over 50 years ago as a general forum for those involved in the administration of pension funds. It has developed to the extent that it is now recognised as a major spokesman for pension funds, particularly in negotiations and consultations with the Government, the Inland Revenue, the DHSS and the OPB. It has a central Council, with a small permanent secretariat at its Croydon office, and has local branches. As well as giving a general information service to members, it organises courses and conferences, and aims to enhance the pensions management profession, particularly through participation in the Pensions Management Institute, a body established jointly by the NAPF, the Society of Pensions Consultants, the Life Offices Association and the Association of Consulting Actuaries.

In addition, the NAPF is a major publisher in this area. It publishes the following series of Notes on Pensions (the prices given are those for non-members of the NAPF; out-of-print ones are omitted):

No. 2 *Pension Scheme Trusteeship* (£2.10)

No. 3 *Social Security Pensions Act 1975* (£1.50)

No. 5 *Towards Equality in Retirement Ages* (60p)

No. 6 *Joint PRAG Publication: Financial Reports for Pension Funds* (£1.10)

No. 7 *Evidence to the Committee to Review Financial Institutions* (£2.00)

No. 8 *Evidence to the OPB on Solvency and Transferability* (£1.50)

The NAPF also publishes three larger works, which contain much valuable up-to-date material. These are the NAPF Annual Survey of Occupational Pension Schemes (the 1979 survey was published in March 1980, price £10), the NAPF Year Book (the 1980 edition costs £12), and the Handbook on Pensions and Employee Benefits and Companion Volume. This last publication is a major collection of the relevant statutory and other material covering pension schemes, which is kept up-to-date. In 1980 it cost £24, with an annual subscription of £16 for the up-dating service.

5. The Company Pensions Information Centre

The CPIC was set up in 1973 by about 20 insurance companies involved in occupational pensions; it is primarily an advisory and educational body, though as such it works independently of the founding companies and so, for example, is not there to promote the merits of fully insured schemes alone. They will provide speakers for a wide range of audiences, including trade unions who wish to become active in this field, provide written articles on pensions, and will give answers to questions concerning *general* information (though it must be stressed that they are *not* brokers or consultants). Also, they publish a series of booklets which are aimed at basic pensions education for the layman. These booklets are:

How a pension fund works (November 1976)

What is a pension fund trustee? (October, 1977)

How to explain your pension scheme (Janaury 1978)
How to understand your pension scheme (February 1978)
Pensions for women (March 1978)
How changing jobs affects your pension (February 1979)

Single copies may be obtained free by sending a stamped self-addressed envelope (at least 7" x 9") to the CPIC; larger orders are charged at 20p per copy.

6. The Equal Opportunities Commission

The EOC is of course interested in occupational pension schemes, from the angle of equal treatment for men and women, as was seen in Chapter 9. It has made written replies to consultative documents produced by the DHSS, and articles by the Chairman of the EOC, Baroness Lockwood, on sex equality in pension schemes can be found in Pensions Review (Summer 1979) and Pensions World (June 1979, at p. 320). The EOC has also published booklets on *Sex equality and the pension age* (1977), *Equalising the pension age* (1978) and *Response to the DHSS Consultative Document "A Happier Old Age"* (1979).

7. The Trades Union Congress

As we saw in Chapter 7, the TUC sees pension funds as a necessary area for trade union involvement. The views of the TUC are fully set out in "Occupational Pension Schemes: a TUC guide" (February 1976; 50p). A new edition of this guide is being prepared, with a view to publication late in 1980. Also, the Handbook on Pensions and Employee Benefits (mentioned above when dealing with the NAPF) contains a section by the General Secretary of the TUC, which might be consulted.

8. The Confederation of British Industry

While the CBI welcomed the Social Security Pensions Act 1975 as an end to pensions being treated as something of a political football, it was opposed (see Chap. 7) to further proposals to make 50 per cent. union control compulsory. Some of its publications have therefore been devoted to its opposition to these proposals. Booklets published by the CBI include:

Guidance on provision of information to members of occupational pension schemes (July 1973; 45p).

Social Security Pensions Act 1975: guidance for employers (July 1976: £1).

Who should manage pension schemes? (May 1977; 50p).

Participation by members in the management of occupational pensions schemes: a guide to good practice (October 1977: £1.50).

Further Reading

Although this book has attempted to give only an overall view of occupational pension schemes and their importance in the industrial relations context, it will have been obvious that they are surrounded by a lot of complicated, detailed law. Anyone needing to look into such detail may gain assistance from the following books:

Ellison, *Private Occupational Pension Schemes* (Oyez, 1979; 2 vols).

Hosking's Pension Schemes and Retirement Benefits (Sweet & Maxwell, 4th ed. 1977).

Jackson, *Occupational Pensions—the New Law* (New Commercial Publishing Co., 1977).

Lucas, *Pensions and Industrial Relations* (Pergamon Press, 1977).

In addition, the reader should consult the Notes of Guidance on Occupational Pension Schemes (IR.12) issued by the Inland Revenue Superannuation Funds Office. Additional detailed legal information may be found in the following official publications (obtainable from HMSO):

Solvency, Disclosure of Information and Member Participation in Occupational Pension Schemes (Cmnd. 5904, February 1975; 3 vols).

White Paper—The Role of Members in the Running of Schemes (Cmnd. 6514, June 1976).

Equal Status for Men and Women in Occupational Pension Schemes (Cmnd. 6599, August 1976).

Occupational Pension Scheme Cover for Disabled People (Cmnd. 6849, June 1977).

Occupational Pensions Board Annual Report.

Index